I0796512

A Design Journey

Tara Bernerd

A Design Journey
Tara Bernerd

Text by Becky Sunshine

龍津美食
早餐

Preface by Tara Bernerd

Design for me is a journey, one that is never ending. With each place I travel to, another story unfolds. It appears at odds with what I do to say that design should be invisible, but let me explain: Good design transports us without us being entirely conscious of the fact. It's an osmosis, a texture, an attitude, the way light might affect us. It's a place we don't want to leave, somewhere we feel a soulful connection to, but maybe we can't put into words why or what that is. Something that resonates deeply. That's what I mean by invisible design.

I'm obsessed with how one feels in a place. If you can take someone out of their day-to-day life—be it because they've come for dinner, for an aperitivo, or they've booked a trip—and something you've designed can alter how they feel, to me that is extraordinary.

I grew up knowing I had a creative, curious, and passionate purpose that meant I needed to explore; to challenge myself and others, to see as much of the world as I could and meet as many people and experience as many cultures as possible. This book is a marker of my journey in life and in my work to date. My career as a designer has become my passport to living and helps quench my thirst for knowledge, adventure, and perspective. Crucially, collaboration is at the core and forms the foundation of how we work at my studio. We seek to find new perspectives, acquire wisdom by telling stories, coming together to listen, to exchange and develop ideas and see what might emerge. My aim is to create meaningful, timeless, and seductive spaces that will linger in someone's mind and heart.

Creating this book matters enormously to me. Within its pages, I can reflect on the journey that each project has taken me on, and the orchestra of talents required to make our ideas a reality. My collaborators, my family and friends, my mentors, my clients, and those who inspire me are part of this journey too. We're all storytellers and together our concepts and experiences, these relationships I cherish deeply, are part of that journey. I am immensely proud of what we have accomplished and am delighted to share our latest work with you. My hope is that this book transports you too, takes you on a journey of your own, and enriches your life—as my ongoing adventures enrich mine.

P.6 Gstaad; Tara at Mirage House by Doug Aitken; Wanchai street life

こだま
KODAMA
新大阪
Shin-Osaka

Foreword
by Tyler Brûlé

This story starts at a dinner in Mayfair in the mid 1990s. It's a swank setting in a subterranean dining room, the crowd is chic, there's a buzz that's the best of London with just enough New York. If memory serves, there was a bit of Hong Kong in the mix as well. It was all on point and when I look back was a perfect representation of all I loved about that decade. Beside me was a chic young woman who took me under her wing and for the entire eve we chatted about magazines and designers we admired, restaurants we respected, hotels that were second homes, and a few places that might need a refresh. I remember walking out on to Berkeley Square feeling both lucky and energized to have spent hours with someone so delightfully sharp, witty but also hugely positive. That we shared the same initials was something that would eventually launch countless conversations of a luxury powerhouse. More on that another day.

For nearly three decades I have met Tara Bernerd in places where we've found inspiration and opportunities. I've shown her my Tokyo, and worked with my colleagues on her visual identity. I have also had a front-row seat as she has grown from that aspiring designer over dinner to a creative force at the top of her game. While this volume is a necessary chronicle of projects completed for the finest owners, brands, and partners, for me it's a marker of achievement, curiosity, but above all friendship. If you've not met the woman behind this book, make it a life's mission to spend a decadent evening with her, just as I did. If you know Tara then you will no doubt recognize much of what I've said and why there must, at some point, be a cinematic version of a life that's been dedicated to the creation of environments that lift moods, coddle, and remind us why it's good to flirt.

P.8 Tyler Brûlé and Tara Bernerd, Tokyo, 2008

Introduction

True creatives are fascinating people to understand. What inspires and motivates them, and what leads them to their artistic conclusions? Tara Bernerd is a true creative, compelled to design, to make and collaborate, inspired by all that's around her. Her curiosity and imagination are constant. Intuition is a driver, too: Knowing what a place should be, how it should function, how it might occupy someone's senses as they engage and navigate; and how interior architecture and design must acknowledge its broader environmental context. Bernerd is adept at it all. Her strength lies in the power of collective creativity, responding to the magic that comes from visionaries brought together, pooling skills and concepts to produce something extraordinary.

Part of what propels Bernerd is a desire to challenge what design should be—specifically hotel design, the main concern of this book—and to show what's possible, to take people away from their quotidian lives and on a journey of discovery, to push their boundaries and expectations a little, be they clients or guests. The impetus lies in Bernerd really knowing her audience, even being that person herself—a discerning, cultured, global citizen with a thirst for adventure and experience. There's a profound understanding of the true definition of luxury. Like her, visitors to her spaces appreciate the multi-layered storytelling through ideas in design, and how she establishes the tone of a place through architectural flow and layout, through light, color, texture, and furniture curation.

Bernerd's spaces are warm and inviting, feeling rooted in location—perhaps that's the red thread. There are unexpected bold gestures in material and palettes, in the curation of art and fine craft, in surprising material combinations, and in furniture—predominantly custom-designed for each interior. There is always a reassuring sense of serenity and practicality in a Tara Bernerd space. However, her work goes much deeper than decoration and efficiency. She manages, through the expression of her design, to create an atmosphere of cultured sophistication, a deliciously stylish version of sexiness which leads us, her guests, to an inexorable feeling that we're in the right place with the right people at the right time.

P.10 Tara, Forte dei Marmi; Ting Kau Bridge, Hong Kong; Julien Desselle Paris home; Hotel Pitrizza, Sardinia

Look for the autobiographical details in Bernerd's work and the clues are there. A good deal comes from her own formative years and professional life of extensive international travel, a lifetime's exposure to cultures other than her own, to countries, people, architecture, hospitality, and crucially, new definitions of luxury. Bernerd's memory for detail is thrilling too, understanding how every encounter might contain the essence of something that could find its way into a Tara Bernerd project. Perhaps it's the sense of arrival at La Voile d'Or, a favorite Cap-Ferrat hotel she visited regularly as a child, or the electricity that washes over her as she arrives in Hong Kong—its vibrancy, noise, the skyline at night, and the buzz of glamorous people at glamorous dinners. Perhaps it's the decadence of cocktails with friends at the Chateau Marmont, the sweeping curves of southern California's mid-century buildings, the raw, sun-soaked hues of a Luis Barragán house in Mexico, or the industrial modernism of Pierre Chareau's Maison de Verre in Paris. It's all there—those experiences and recollections, those influences distilled as a new perspective that later becomes the kernel of an idea.

A Design Journey serves as a companion to Bernerd's first book, *Place* (published in 2017), and explores the evolution of her award-winning interior architecture and design practice, Tara Bernerd & Partners, founded in 2002. Connecting both these volumes—and ultimately what underlines the studio's DNA—is a unique approach and sensibility that inhabits each project. What's evolved since the publication of *Place* is the ambition, complexity, and scale of projects.

The eleven projects included in this book are an opportunity to reflect on and make sense of the studio's diverse and significant accomplishments. Through examining Bernerd's design and process, it leads us to understand what motivates someone to leap on a plane, to go to that place, to explore, escape, indulge, and build lifelong memories—to reveal the journey. Power lies in Bernerd's innate ability to create meaning in design; playing with how people experience her spaces. And, just as she intends, a Tara Bernerd–designed interior will always feel just a little bit yours, like a home away from home.

P.12 Børge Mogensen chair; Jeanloup Sieff for *Harper's Bazaar*; Villa Can Cocotero
P.14 Fiat Giardiniera at TWA Hotel, New York; Maison de Verre, Paris; Walt Disney Concert Hall, Los Angeles; Gstaad

P.15 Asakura House, Shibuya; Barcelona doorway; Fungo lamp; Porsche 911

"The essence of travel is to be moved. This feels increasingly relevant as the world homogenizes, to be able to savor the tastes of each place. Travel should be special: the moment you arrive somewhere the scent of a new, foreign place, absorbing the atmosphere, the culture, new experiences."

P.16 Griffith Observatory, Los Angeles; Lake Como; Tara in Mexico; Sculpture House by Jacques Couëlle

Tara Bernerd Projects

Rosewood Munich

Much of Munich's beauty centers on the elegance and vitality of its Old Town, where the Rosewood Hotel, the vision of the Schörghuber family of Bayerische Hausbau, is situated. The first major project in Germany for the studio, its inspiration flows from the city's blend of stately baroque architecture, its ultra-modern inventions, and vibrant Bavarian culture. The hotel's ornate façade and foyer are all that remain of the former State Bank of Bavaria and the adjacent residence, the Palais Neuhaus-Preysing. The restored entrance is immediately at odds with the bustling city outside with its soaring ceiling, the sweep of the stone stairs, and the juxtaposition of contemporary design pieces. It's serene and sophisticated, where lighting is soft and the gentle flow of layout suggests the discovery of what lies ahead as one ascends the stairs into the hotel's reception, a sumptuous living room with public spaces beyond. This is the place for *Gemütlichkeit*—a feeling of coziness and conviviality, a respite for the well-heeled, well-seasoned traveler. It's also a place where high-level business is done, meetings that might morph from elegant lunches to sunset cocktails and long dinners. Rooting the hotel in Munich, there are connections to the Bavarian landscape and craftsmanship everywhere—a forest-like palette, graphic patterns, textured joinery and stonemasonry by German master craftspeople. The contemporized, vaulted ceilings of the below-ground spa reference the cellars of German castles. The Wintergarten, a focal point, faces a lush central courtyard with warm-toned seating and roaring fireplaces, celebrating all that is stylish about travel. There's mastery in the flow, effortlessly transporting guests from public spaces to the 59 suites, 73 rooms and five residences. Each is a visual feast with exquisite detailing in flooring, timber paneling, and artwork. Rooms feel handsome and substantial, each with a living area. Furniture and fittings, mostly designed in-house, are free-standing, allowing for multiple layouts while also feeling luxuriously residential.

P.20 Main entrance to the hotel, originally the State Bank of Bavaria

SCHALTER
HOF
TRESOR

SCHÄLTER
HOF
TRESOR

HOMES FOR OUR TIME
bauhaus

"Our design at Rosewood Munich needed in my mind to embrace the city's rich history, but equally speak to Munich today. The city is energetic and incredibly elegant and it was important to me that the flavor was reflected in our work."

P. 22 The entrance lobby features a 3D-printed, polished plaster and marble porter station designed by Tara Bernerd
P. 24 Upholstered armchair, footstool, and petrol-blue lacquered side table designed by Tara Bernerd

"Attention to detail was a pivotal part of the design. The selection of stone was extensive, which played a huge part in the interior. Working with local craftsmen we were able to celebrate artisanal skills in our furniture, which transcended into each fabric chosen throughout the property."

P.26 Reception living room with custom-designed concierge desk and stone floor inspired by the building's original flooring. The diamond grid motif in the ceiling references the Bavarian state flag
P.29 Petrol-blue sofa, armchair and coffee table designed by Tara Bernerd

100 INTERIORS AROUND THE WORLD
Moderne Kunst
FRITZ KAHN

"The principal idea was to create a home, albeit a rather grand home, that celebrated the Bavarian warmth and hospitality that I'd come to know during our time working there. From a fireplace in the Wintergarten to rooms and suites that reflected a stylish home of today."

P.30 The Wintergarten custom-designed double-sided marble fireplace faces the outdoor central courtyard
P.32 Handcrafted bronze and opal glass chandelier suspended over the communal table designed by Tara Bernerd

5
4
3
2
1
LG

OTO
SPA

P.43 Nido armchair by Sancal
in bespoke finish
P.44 Nesting tables crafted in
Calacatta Oro marble, blue lacquer,
and timber with marquetry inlay
P.45 Bespoke timber, two-sided
bookshelf with smoked glass

P.46 Built-in joinery blends timber, leather, and bronzed metal with mirrored inset panels. The sofa and stone coffee table are custom designed
P.47 A Bavarian bar clad with inset tiles and stone top, with saddle-leather bar stools, is central to the in-room pantry

P.51 Oversized bed with suede and curved leather headboard. Bronzed metal and timber shelving and patterned rug are bespoke pieces. Ensuite bathroom features vanity station and floating shelf, both in Verde marble

JONATHAN BECKER 30 YEARS at VANITY FAIR
BECKER 30 YEARS AT VANITY FAIR

THE WOODBOOK
MERT ALAS & MARCUS PIGGOTT
Design
arts & architecture
CALATRAVA
LOGO MODERNISM
HOMES FOR OUR TIME

"Hong Kong is the city that really never sleeps. The buzz and energy are invigorating and exciting, as are the people. The hotel is an oasis in the midst of this incredible metropolis. Bold design, strong colors, and lifestyle were essential to integrate into our design."

P.59–60 Bar is custom designed in local Ming green marble. Fluted glass sliding panels and linen laminated glass offer privacy and diffused lighting

Maker's Mark
KNOB CREEK

"Aron Harilela, our client and my dear friend, is the embodiment of chic. Colors and materials here reflect Hong Kong's design savvy and Aron's own eye for detail. There is spirit and personality throughout the hotel and striking architectural details, such as the ceiling at Zoku."

P. 62 Bespoke blue velvet sofa and armchair in suede and linen, and graphic rug designed by Tara Bernerd

THE ILLUSTRATOR
FRENCH RIVIERA
LOGO MODERNISM
Circle of Love
ALBERT OEHLEN

S IS FOR STYLE
BENTLEY

P.65 Green polished plaster walls offset Costa Smeralda granite and Bianco Lasa marble flooring and walls in the main powder room

ENOC PEREZ
lisa perry

"I like to entertain, I like to go out. So how do you create something that is going to ignite? How are you going to make someone feel a sense of home, somewhere that they can sit back but also somewhere that seduces? Those are the things that are key to the bars and public areas of a hotel. We then create tranquility and peace where we lay our heads."

P.66 Zoku restaurant features an oak origami ceiling, banquettes in pink leather and highlight fabric, graphic rug by Tara Bernerd and khaki linen and walnut dining chairs
P.69 Booth screened by bronze and fluted glass screen

"The guest rooms and suites were designed as a retreat from the energy of the public areas of the hotel and the city itself. While the color and material palette feel serene and very refined, we've created vistas that remind you that you're in one of the most dynamic places on earth."

P.72 Terrace runs the length of the room, offering views across the city
P.75 Guest suite with blue corduroy headboard, bespoke walnut and glass-top nightstand and bespoke rug

P.76–77 Bathrooms clad in Calacatta Oro marble, custom-designed mirrors to reflect natural light. Contrasting hardware is antique bronze

36
EUROPE

P.78 Bedroom suite with oak wall paneling, bronze framed glass dividing door to bathroom

Maroma, a Belmond Hotel

Often the soul and authenticity of a project is embedded in its wider locale. The richness of the Yucatán landscape—its dense, lush jungle, golden coastline, and the cacophony of native wildlife, all of it a love letter to its environment—springs to life with the design at Maroma, owned by Belmond Hotels. Excitement builds before reaching the palapa-style villas of the hotel—a long private drive sets the scene before you glimpse what was once the sprawling 1970s residence of architect Jose Luis Moreno. What's there now honors its breathtaking natural scenery while paying tribute to the laidback, glamorous vibe of the property's former existence. Here, in a Mexican debut for the studio, the many sources of inspiration are found on the 72-room hotel's doorstep: the textures, colors, flavors, and energy of the region. The landscape and culture are given a new expression in the redesign, with local materials, the sun-drenched color palette, and beautifully handmade details in furniture and fittings, all of it designed in-house and fabricated locally. Creating harmonious layout and flow are Bernerd trademarks; here they are used specifically to maximize the vistas at every turn. The lobby now has views directly to the beach; a new glazed façade in the restaurant sends swathes of natural light through the space, as well as offering unrestricted views of the sea, enjoyed from every vantage point, especially newly created stepped seating. Utilizing every recess is another studio forte, creating cozy corners that transform themselves from relaxing, serene spaces by day to sophisticated hotspots by night—and Freddy's Bar, the reimagined pool bar, does just that. One can sense the spirit of the fabulous guests of the 1970s and 1980s, stylish and seductive. Elsewhere, maximizing floorplates by reconfiguring rooms and suites has also created an opportunity for increased connectivity between spaces, while the new beachfront suites are the latest sensitive architectural addition that feel as if they've been there for decades.

P.80 Hotel entrance with bespoke pebble patterned floor and handcrafted chandelier

P.82 Rattan pocket doors in Pool Bar lounge. Curved sofa, ottoman and tables designed by Tara Bernerd
P.85 Raffia panels in the Pool Bar, parota timber coffee table made locally
P.86 Bespoke carved timber loungers upholstered in striped linen. Umbrellas developed with Tucci, custom side tables with glazed lava stone tops and iron bases made locally

"Every single material has been carefully considered to connect to the landscape and the culture of the region. The heritage of textiles, craft, and use of color has been embedded into the design, the tactility, and the soul of this place."

P.89 View to Woodend restaurant with onyx-clad kitchen. Each vestibule shows glazed ceramic tiles; the mosaic floor tiles, and bespoke planters, custom designed by Tara Bernerd

P.90 Seating in Woodend restaurant, marble-topped tables and bespoke mosaic floor all by Tara Bernerd
P.92 Bespoke chandeliers made by local artisan Kublaikan with shell beading and bronze metal frame
P.94 Bespoke lava stone topped dining table with carved pedestal base
P.95 Bespoke carved timber dining table with tile top and carved timber chairs
P.96 Custom pebble border inspired by traditional Mexican motifs
P.97 Custom coffee tables with inset stone tops and hand-carved borders at Freddy's Bar. Seating crafted from local stone with inlaid pebble detailing

P.100 Custom carved timber bar front with Verde Guatemala marble top at the Pool Bar. Patterned ceramic floor tiles are handcrafted locally
P.102 Rooftop terrace with bespoke parasol and hand-carved sunlounger
P.104 Bespoke curved and carved timber sofa with linen upholstery, ottoman and woven jute rug all made in Mexico. Handcrafted parota coffee table with live edge. Timber and mosaic dining table by Tara Bernerd with carved ceramic pendant light above

"One of the most spectacular things about Maroma is how it layers together: From the sea to the sand, the jungle, the sounds, and scents. We've linked every piece of furniture, every fixture and all the lighting to its environment and its origins as a home."

P.107 Bespoke carved timber sofa with integrated side table, woven jute rug made in Mexico
P.108 Private bar in villa lounge with traditional stained-timber door panels

P.109 Suite with palapa roof, bespoke tiles. Bench with woven rattan is handcrafted locally
P.110 Travertine dressing table inset between rattan-front wardrobes with hand-carved door handles

P.112 Signature suite with woven cane headboard set within a plastered arched niche, hand-painted timber bedside tables. Local Mexican fabrics used for accent cushions
P.114–115 Oversized carved stone tub in guest bathroom. Double vanities with Tarahumara stone counters and locally hand-carved timber. Hand-painted motif around the room; saltillo and white tiled floor and hand-blown glass wall lights both made locally

“To be positioned this close to the ocean is a rare gift. At every turn we were prioritizing vistas: beautiful places to pause, to be quiet and contemplative, but equally, places to socialize, to come together. The key was placing these subtle reminders of locale through a rich tapestry of materials, pattern, and color.”

P.116 Guestroom terrace with traditional palapa roof and uninterrupted views of the sea. Flooring is bespoke, with pebble inlay and organic timber railings. Mosaic stone-top dining table and handcrafted cane chairs are made locally
P.118 The main palapa offers a first glimpse of the beach ahead

P.120–121 The hotel spa apothecary with central carved stone, counter on inlaid pebble floor, inspired by melipona beehive patterns. Ceramic pendants designed by Heather Levine. Room outlined with crafted timber shelving to display tinctures

Conrad Los Angeles

In the regenerated downtown Los Angeles, an energetic creative community meets the business world; architecture ranges from hi-tech skyscrapers to heritage buildings, and verdant pockets punctuate the urban landscape with the Hollywood sign in the distance. Adjacent to Frank Gehry's landmark Walt Disney Concert Hall is The Grand LA, a mixed-use venue, also by Gehry. From the eighth floor up it's the Conrad Los Angeles hotel, the brainchild of Stephen Ross and Ken Himmel of Related Ross, with interior architecture and design by Tara Bernerd. A new building—a blank canvas—can be a gift, as is working with the monumental scale and radical form of the concert hall. From the tenth-floor arrival, vistas of the hall's bold, stainless-steel sail-like structure are seen through dramatic floor-to-ceiling glazing. Where dynamic volumes and reflective materials live outside, the inside is intimate and warm. Bernerd takes what is expansive and makes it human scale through movement and light. Guests are guided from the living-room-style reception zone with custom seating that delivers a 1970s nightlife quality, with a bespoke tiled fireplace, through to a main bar area with timber chandeliers, leading to the restaurants, a sculptural champagne bar, a wrap-around sunset terrace and pool deck. Southern California's mid-century aesthetic appears as geometric patterns in both textiles and tiling; sculptural ceiling juts recall the waves of the concert hall. The color palette reflects the landscape with added denim-blue accents, while the rawness of stone used across the reception and concierge desks and elevator area contrasts the shine of metallics, smooth polished concrete and the rich upholstery and drapery. Modernity meets old Hollywood glamour in the 305 guest rooms and suites. Studio-designed oversized headboards, wardrobes and beds, the flexibility of sliding walls which reveal bathrooms counterbalance with a more contemporary design for a timeless feel.

P.126 Custom designed Ceppo di Gré stone reception desk with brushed oak detailing; privacy screen made with distressed steel with integrated lighting

"The architecture of this building — and, of course, the Walt Disney Concert Hall right next to it — is monumental. The scale and reflections of both structures are utterly magnificent, so I wanted our silhouettes and material palette to have a direct dialogue."

P.129 Bespoke Ceppo di Gré carved concierge niche with timber detailing. Walnut fluted coffee tables designed by Tara Bernerd. Lounge chairs with leather arms and woven upholstery

P.130–131 Bespoke arrivals banquette designed by Tara Bernerd, upholstered in indigo cotton linen; coffee tables with fumed oak legs and limestone top; ottomans are customized with zigzag fabric and stained-walnut base

Peter Lindbergh
CALATRAVA

P.133 Fluted glazed white ceramic wall tiles by Inax; Henge lights are customized in a burnished brass finish
P.134 Ceppo stone walls and timber finials over bronzed mirror in the Beaudry Room bar
P.136 Custom travertine bar side table

"We wanted the interior to honor the architecture, so blending the two was paramount. That meant drawing down ceiling volumes in organic forms, maximizing vistas at every turn and adding warmth with rich materials. The space also needed furniture with attitude."

P.137–139 Main bar top is crafted in Pyrolave with bespoke profile detailing
P.141–143 Main bar area features a bespoke bar sofa in rust corduroy and chestnut leather seating; bespoke patterned floor tiles are handmade in California. Side tables have a rough travertine finish. Rattan and upholstered armchairs are by Bonacina

P.145 Terrace with views of the Walt Disney Concert Hall. Quartzite tables and sofa are bespoke
P.147–149 The restaurant is screened by a fluted glass divider; the bespoke banquette is designed by Tara Bernerd with green velvet and leather

P.151 Suspended back-bar is crafted in distressed steel and timber shelving with glass inserts and integrated lighting. Bespoke Caesarstone bar top with Pyrolave bar front tiles. Custom oak and leather bar stools

"Both inside and out I wanted interconnected reminders of southern California's landscape. By introducing abundant planting, which is beautifully lit by night, and shady nooks for seating outside, the rawness of woven fabrics and the warmth of timber furniture, you know exactly where you are."

P.153 – 154 Restaurant terrace trellis designed by Frank Gehry in Douglas fir; bespoke ceramic tile-top dining tables designed by Tara Bernerd. Wicker pendant lights and bar stools are customized, both by Palacek

P.156–157 Pool cabana textured terracotta tiles made locally, the sofas designed by Tara Bernerd
P.158 Natural teak loungers with striped linen upholstery and green glazed ceramic mushroom stools at rooftop pool

"We used European oak as paneling for warmth and had fun with tactile, colorful upholstery and muted, brushed metals as accents. Introducing contemporary art was a way of rooting us in Los Angeles as it is now."

P.161 Brushed-oak wall panels throughout penthouse dining and living area. Dining table with walnut legs and travertine top and console both by Tara Bernerd
P.162 Green corduroy sofa in penthouse living room, walnut floor lamp with linen shade. Walnut framed armchair by Gio Ponti

Tara Bernerd · Place
Peter Lindbergh

P.164–165 Curved kitchen island in the penthouse crafted in brushed oak with Caesarstone top; bar stools are walnut

KUMA

"We created an open, pared-back concept for the guest rooms and suites, using reflection and movement to activate each space. We designed bespoke beds, headboards, sofas, lighting, and wardrobes for each room — all of it feels striking and timeless. There's an air of mid-century seduction in there too."

P.166 Grey marble console sits at entrance of grand penthouse, lined with oak-panelled walls
P.168 Walls lined with geometric oak paneling; floor-to-ceiling brushed brass lamp with linen shade, bespoke sofa and brushed oak dining table with glass top all by Tara Bernerd
P.169 Bedroom and bathroom separated by bespoke sliding wall partition with bronze-tinted frosted glass and brushed metalwork

CALATRAVA
KUMA

“Even the smallest details that connect areas of a hospitality space enable us to tell one coherent story. At Conrad Los Angeles we’ve achieved that with bespoke elements and a consistent palette of materials, paying homage to walkways and celebrating every space.”

P.170 Relaxation room with bespoke designed cerused oak with travertine vanity unit

Frette and Medea 1905

At the heart of the studio's design journey lies an ongoing dialogue with material, form, and craft. It tells the story not only of those who have designed the furniture, lighting, and accessories that shape each project, but of the skilled craftspeople who bring each piece to life. These relationships, cultivated over years of collaboration with a network of artisans and fabricators, are central to the studio's ethos, particularly in its partnerships with heritage Italian houses Frette and Medea 1905. The result is work that reflects Bernerd's most enduring instincts, grounded in the experience of the studio designing hotels, private residences, and hospitality spaces. For Frette, renowned for its linens and home accessories, Bernerd created Disrupting Architecture, a collection of cushions and throws inspired by early modernist patterns from around the world, celebrating Deco buildings such as Eltham Palace and the Carlyle Hotel, and New York's iconic architecture. Each piece draws from architectural elements, abstracted through color, geometry and repetition, woven in cashmere and wool. For Medea 1905, the collection comprises eight pieces designed for living, dining, and sleeping, envisioned as standalone forms but curated to work cohesively. A sculptural chaise is inspired by Sardinia's weather-worn rock formations; a bed recalls bygone glamour in high-gloss walnut and rattan (a nod to mid-century surfaces); a drinks cabinet glows from within, lined in marble, glass, and leather. Most pieces are framed in timber, with sweeping blades and curves that give each a sense of weight and presence; confident silhouettes, sculptural forms, and a subtle interplay between softness and structure. The material palette—oak, walnut, marble, lacquer, leather—is tactile and enduring, designed to age beautifully. For both collections, which were exhibited together, each of these pieces feels personal, a natural extension of the rooms created by the studio, the collaborators, and the process that has guided Bernerd to explore, edit, evolve.

P.172 Disrupting Architecture cushions and throws by Tara Bernerd for Frette
P.174 Medea 1905 chair by Tara Bernerd with Modernism throw and cushions

"The collection begins with form and from there individualism arrives. Each piece is unique, each with its own voice, allowing a natural reaction to a mood, a place, and a lifestyle."

P.176 Deco throw cushions with Modernism cushion
P.177 Volpe chaise with Deco throw and cushions
P.179 Luigi cocktail bar with antique brass, leather handle and marble top

"I'm quite bold in what I do. I like something that's strong. For this collection I thought about my travels and experiences. There's a nod to the glamour of the past while embracing the artisans of today. This has been a journey of celebrating people's memories, their movement and shape."

P.180 Lola bed with Modernism and Deco throw and cushions

Villa Can Cocotero Ibiza

There is a particular kind of magic that exists in Ibiza—a spirituality embedded in the landscape. Hidden away in the west of the island, with the pine-covered mountains behind and the Mediterranean Sea ahead, is the sprawling Villa Can Cocotero. The villa—its minimal exterior designed by Spanish architect Jordi Carreño, with interiors by Tara Bernerd—is part of the 42-acre private Sabina Estate, the vision of Anton Bilton. Bernerd's work seeks to be sensitive and responsive, creating a clear visual language that references the energy and nature of its location, as well as considering who will occupy the space. From the structure of the six-bedroom house—its simple, linear single-story form clad in Ibiza stone and a vibrant creep of bougainvillea—to its haven interior and gardens, there's a constant connection to the island's raw otherworldliness. Materiality begins at the villa's entrance, the warmth of the Iroko front door opening into the main living space, with uninterrupted views of the private gardens and pool with the sea beyond. Keen to maintain the open, airy stretch of the living area, layers of interest appear as texture and curated furniture, including custom, vintage, and contemporary pieces for a sense of intimacy. Designed for contemplation and relaxation, attention was given to ensuring it was also set up for socializing and entertaining—a home that moves effortlessly from inside to the outdoors through the seasons, achieved in zoning and the use of textures and natural light. Ibiza stone, seen outside, repeats across an internal wall, much like the limestone flooring which has a roughness externally as poolside paving but appears smooth for the indoors. A timber-framed skylight and custom-woven cable baluster cast dynamic shadows down to the lower-level entertainment space that features a pool table area, bespoke bar, wine store, and screening room. The bedroom suites are designed with a constant connection to the outdoors too: bathrooms feature reflective surfaces and finely honed marble basins, while bedrooms provide serenity and sanctity with warm shades of timber in the joinery and deep window seats.

P.182 Teak sun loungers are placed in the private garden by the pool

"There's an incredible energy in Ibiza I wanted to honor. To bring in the rawness and texture that you feel throughout the island — just think of the arid landscape, the scent of pine trees, the lavender everywhere. We used the rough Ibiza stone from the façade across a wall inside and the limestone from the pool area was cut for the salon flooring."

P.184 Pool at rear of the villa is planted with olive trees, pines, and lavender
P.186 – 189 Custom front door is designed with oversized dovetail hinges and House of Eroju door handles. Views directly through the villa to garden and landscape beyond. The house is clad in local Ibiza stone and deep timber-framed windows. Flooring is honed limestone

P.191 Kitchen revealed through smoked cognac Crittal doors; walls are hand-finished stucco plaster, skylight is shaded by oak screen. Rug and pendant light are designed by Tara Bernerd
P.192 Cantilever stairs with vintage-inspired metal and wire banister lead to the lower level entertainment area

KATHARINA GROSSE

P.194 Walls clad in local Ibiza stone. Custom limestone fireplace on far wall
P.195 Kitchen connects to dining area through smoked cognac Crittal doors with views to garden and pool

KATHARINA GROSSE
ARTE
MARK ROTHKO
JOAN MIRÓ
SALVADOR DALÍ
TASCHEN

P.198 Gallery window seats with washed linen upholstery in guest rooms; oversized American oak line the floors, with unlined linen curtains for softness
P.201 Ensuite bathrooms feature patterned-tile flooring and mirrored surfaces. Wardrobes built in American oak with slatted doors

Four Seasons Hotel and Residences, Fort Lauderdale

The sprawl of ocean, expanse of sky, and the sweep of perfect coastline make Florida's landscape feel like nowhere else. The Four Seasons Hotel in Fort Lauderdale, owned by Fort Partners, is set within the ship-like contemporary beachfront building by architect Kobi Karp, with interior architecture and design by Tara Bernerd. The monumental structure encapsulates Fort Lauderdale's evolution, with its historically eclectic architecture, the world's biggest yacht show, and a discerning international crowd. Inside the hotel's lobby and beyond, design cues reference the city's undercurrent of 1960s French Riviera chic and tropical modernism through the color and material palette. A Bernerd interior is often defined by a restrained sophistication that makes visitors question whether an environment is old or new. That's the aim here, too: A fluid relationship between interiors and environment, strong in character, generous in proportions but on a human scale, inviting, subtle, with aesthetic references that are both fresh and familiar. Bernerd has created multiple lines of vision for both the first- and second-floor public areas—a mise-en-scène of grouped furniture and free-standing shelving, with interludes of planting inside and out that recall a residential living room and garden. An adjoining daytime coffee spot effortlessly morphs into a hangout for sundowners' cocktail hour. A dramatic geometric inlaid travertine floor designed in homage to Gio Ponti serves as a foundation for the warmth and serenity of both the public spaces and guest rooms. The guest rooms and suites, light and bright where views are paramount, pick up both the contemporary and mid-century references in the soft hues, polished walnut finishes, and diffused lighting—all of it custom-designed in-house. The wrap-around leather-inlaid desk that becomes a wardrobe and bar recalls the golden era of luxury liners, while the bespoke freestanding furniture complements with a softening of curved silhouettes. The effect is at once invigorating and calming.

P. 202 Exterior of Four Seasons Hotel and Residences, Fort Lauderdale

P.205 Lobby lined with travertine and timber paneling and custom five-stone modernist-inspired floor. Bespoke chandelier crafted with rope knots and high-gloss walnut frame. Artwork, *A La Playa*, by Nik Wheeler

VINYL

P.206 Bespoke high-gloss walnut bookcase with rattan façade and leather inlay shelves, and marble-top side table designed by Tara Bernerd

"I had this very strong sense of a bygone era of Riviera chic in Fort Lauderdale — there's a huge yachting community here and you can see it in the architecture of the city. I was keen to capture that old-school laidback glamour — reminiscent of the craftsmanship of a Riva boat — but contemporize the interior for today's cultured visitors."

P.209 Bespoke geometric inlaid travertine floor designed by Tara Bernerd

P. 210 Bespoke brass wall mirror, armchair upholstered in blue velvet with white piping and cocktail table in elevator lobby entrance
P. 212 White lacquered tongue and groove panels with walnut trim on walls in Honey Fitz lobby lounge. Nautical-style wall lights, marble topped cocktail tables; leather and fabric upholstered armchairs; bespoke white quartz serving table

SAUNA

P.214–215 Spa changing room clad in white marble; sauna with feature wall of illuminated Himalayan salt bricks

P. 216 White lacquered-timber vanity unit with rattan screen and marble top, white lacquered-timber lockers, mint upholstered vanity stool with rattan backrest, and feature stone mosaic flooring, all designed by Tara Bernerd

"The views of the ocean are incredible, combined with a magical light. We intentionally kept the guest room and suites fresh with a lighter palette. Handcrafted furniture, so bespoke pieces, add a sophisticated layer."

P. 218 – 220 Bespoke cantilever high-gloss walnut desk with leather top and desk chair; chaise in white linen; brass and marble side table and striped rug, also bespoke. Metal desk lamp and floor lamp in high-gloss walnut with linen shade by Tara Bernerd

Tara Bernerd • Place

P. 222 Wardrobe door crafted in high-gloss walnut and rattan, fabric-lined walls of guest room and bespoke bench in blue upholstery with high-gloss walnut legs. Artwork is by photographer Annelie Vandendael

Sanlorenzo SX112

The allure of a beautifully crafted yacht presents ample opportunity for creating a bespoke interior that reflects the sophistication and elegance of a vessel's structure, as well as satisfying the desires of its intended occupants. Drawing on the newness of the Sanlorenzo SX112 model—a 112-foot handcrafted boat able to accommodate ten guests and five crew members—Tara Bernerd partnered with Sanlorenzo's boatyard in Liguria and her clients to create a refined, playful, and highly personal space. Working within the parameters of the boat's fixed external architecture, the studio designed an interior exploring the seductive nature of 1970s jet-set travel, lightly contemporizing it to create an air of laidback timelessness. The boat is where family and friends come together, so controlling the interconnectedness of both the inside and outside means the studio has defined spaces to feel equally sociable and intimate, like a luxurious apartment. There are separate areas for relaxing—large-scale sofas in the main living room, a place for movie nights or singing karaoke, a dining area for family meals, and both inside and external spaces for kids to hang out. The captain's deck, with its custom-designed deep blue banquettes, feels like a family room while parents enjoy sunset cocktails. Bernerd balances the practicality needed on a yacht with a considered design language, exploring how the numerous decks can transition according to activities or times of day—cantilevered platforms house jet-skis, for example, while a bar with raised daybeds and stools has been positioned close by. There are retractable sunroofs and mechanized window treatments, enabling views to be maximized, while the internal floorplate has been maneuvered to capitalize on the quantity of cabins needed for numerous family members. As is a particular studio strength, the layering of materials, pattern, and color builds a personal design story. Where storage is required, bespoke joinery has been handcrafted and fitted. There are woven leathers and inset marble, sculptural units overlaid with shagreen and burnished metal trimmed handles. The key here has been a refined version of versatility, where everything has its place and can be stored away as desired.

P. 226 The rear main deck provides the perfect seating area to capture the view

P.229 Extendable decked platform at the lower deck beach club is used for launching marine vehicles. Folding chairs created for easy storage
P.230 The Flying Bridge has custom banquettes with hidden storage. The roof is retractable, flooring is pale oak

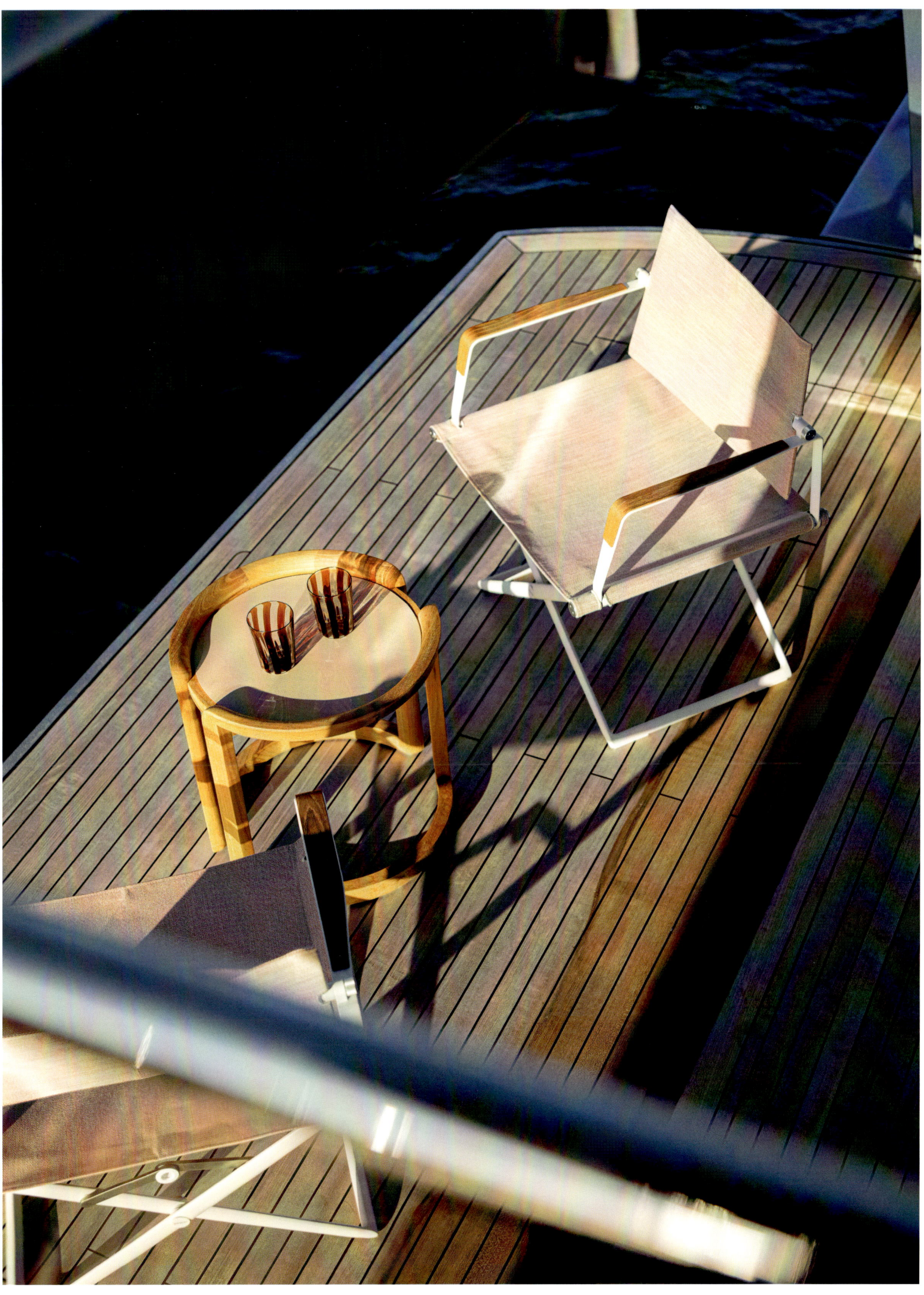

“The boat itself is truly a dynamic piece of design. Therefore, the interior reflected this with a bold, elegant attitude.”

P. 232 Bespoke built-in timber storage cabinets inset with Arabescato Orobico marble and brass-lined woven-leather drawer fronts

Estiatorio Milos West Palm Beach

At the edge of Palm Beach's Intracoastal Waterway is the 25-story glass and burnished white concrete One Flagler tower, a symbol of a revived, vibrant neighborhood with parkland, pedestrianized boulevards, private residences, cafés, and elegant shops. It is here at the base of the building, by architect David Childs of SOM and the vision of developer Related Ross, that renowned chef Costas Spiliadis has opened his Estiatorio Milos, with interiors by Tara Bernerd. The studio is adept at investing in authentic narratives and creating a crafted exchange between place and intent. Bernerd's design responds with quiet confidence to both the setting and the chef's ethos. Across the restaurant's two floors, the design reveals itself with a sense of purpose, grounded in the principles of *philoxenia*—the Greek art of hospitality—and authenticity. Simplicity, understated luxury, with roots in nature. Greek Pentelikon marble, oak, and textured stone echo the landscapes of the Cycladic island of Milos, as does the abundant planting both inside and out. A sculptural staircase at the entrance establishes an architectural focal point, as does the open kitchen and fish market counter. Layout across both floors feels effortless with the introduction of linen-upholstered banquettes, a stone-clad bar and an oak-lined wine store. Upstairs, the connection to the ground floor, shaded terraces and the landscape is evident through the continuum of materiality. Volumes, too, are balanced by the timber bulkhead of the bespoke bar, and the lighting scheme—linen-lined chandeliers designed in-house, ceiling lightwells inspired by Greek rock formations, and wall sconces—casts an ambient glow. The color palette is in restrained sun-bleached neutrals with touches of earthy greens and terracotta, to showcase the food. Instead, layering comes from textural combinations: powdery plaster walls, oak-clad in places to highlight artwork, and columns of fluted plaster handmade on site. A custom reception desk is constructed from ribbons of oak and the gauzy drapery softens the Florida sunlight. Elemental and harmonious, the design maintains a refined elegance.

P.236 Spiral staircase in oak and plaster; integrated lighting elements in the steps and handrail

“The moment I met Costas Spiliadis the room lit up. His energy and passion are inspiring and it has been a privilege to work with him.”

P.239 First-floor dining room with bespoke banquettes in striped linen and oak and wood fiber
P.240 Second-floor custom bar with fluted façade and Pentelikon marble top

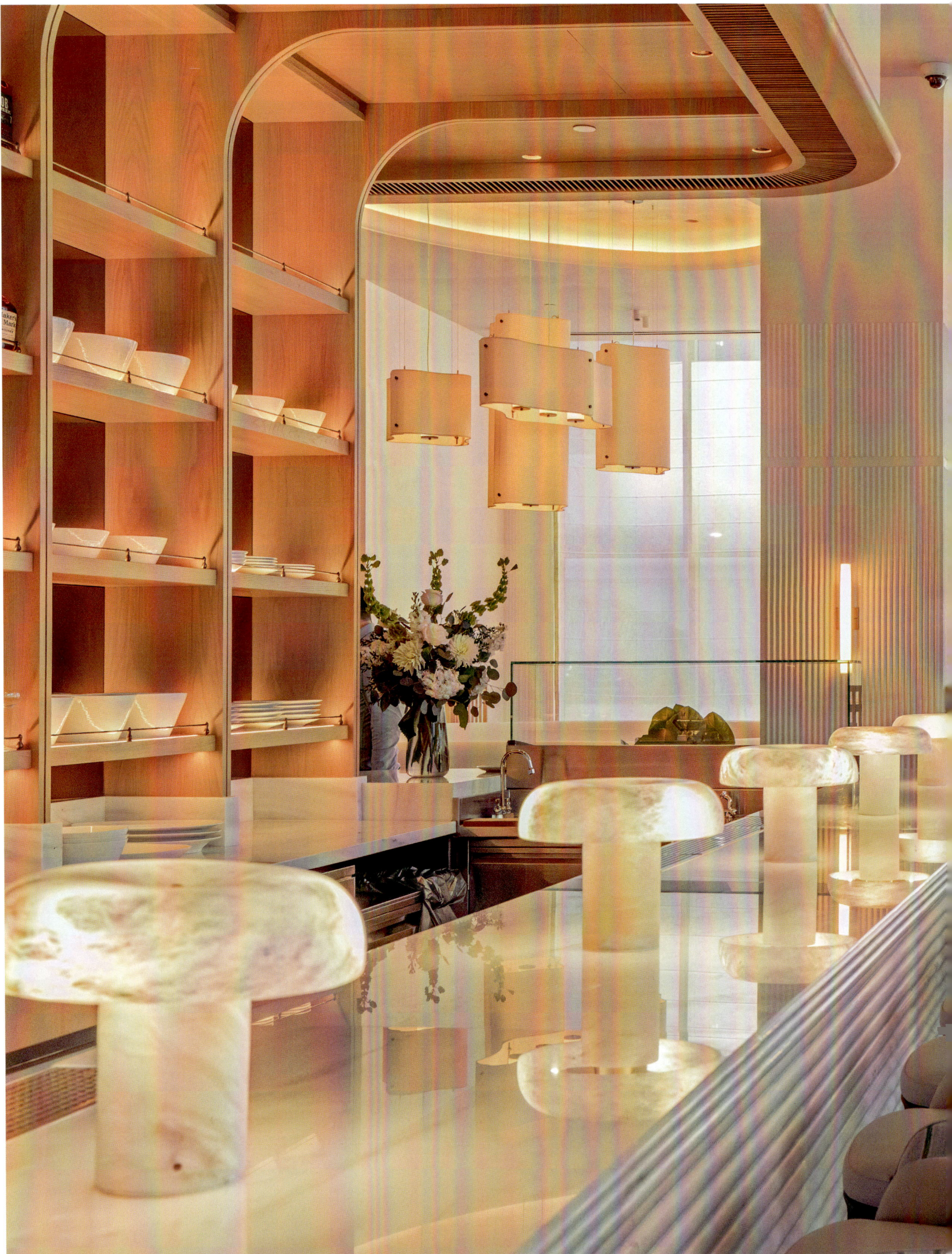

EXIT

"We handled the interiors with the utmost sensitivity, ensuring each space had form, elegance, and warmth. Everything needed to remain a subtle backdrop to the food and embrace its culture and heritage."

P. 243 Handcrafted fluted plaster columns with brass-trimmed wall lights

60 56

P.244 Bespoke wine cellar in oak with Greek marble floor
P.246 The olive tree is central to the main dining area, with views of the wine cellar

Zentis Osaka

Developing a new brand concept is an opportunity not simply to establish a desirable destination but also to bring to life newly crafted stories. For Tara Bernerd's first project in Japan, the studio created both the interior architecture and design at the 212-room Zentis Osaka, owned by Palace Hotel Co Ltd. As a key contributor, Bernerd played a crucial role in defining the hotel's unique rhythm and ambience. The setting—within the commercial district of Dojimahama, busy with office workers by day and by sundown home to a youthful and vibrant nightlife—requires a flexible aesthetic language that can engage both a discerning international crowd and a local audience. The dialogue between a landscaped outside and the interior is exemplified throughout the first floor, where the use of the limed brickwork and blond wood seen on the exterior continues on interior walls and across a bespoke marble-topped reception desk. So too in the gardens, where the studio worked closely with a landscape designer to create a secluded urban oasis; that sense of nature flows through the lobby and lounge where high ceilings and walls of glazing create appealing vistas and a relaxed conviviality. A custom cantilevered stone staircase designed by the studio allows light to flow through its suspended treads. Floor-to-ceiling drapery is sheer and airy, and the room's industrial linear undertones and neutral color palette feel rooted in the contemporary architecture of the building. The lounge has been zoned too to enable people to come together, making connections across a central communal table and adjacent corner seating. Custom-designed upholstered booths along one wall feel intimate and playful, while the integrated backlit shelving enveloping the elevators, timber ceiling beams, and pools of light across the bespoke encaustic-tiled floor are designed to keep the space feeling warm and residential. That laidback sensibility is echoed in the upper-level restaurant and bar areas with a moodier color and material palette, while the guest rooms and suites feel light and calming. Prioritizing space-planning means maximizing floorplates that recall the elemental zoning of a bento box: sliding doors open to corner bathrooms, open joinery, and built-in storage under the seating.

P.248 Reception desk in limestone brick tiles and green marble top; poured concrete floors with geometric grooves

Gerrit Rietveld

“In creating a public space that feels fresh and welcoming, rather than formal and austere, there comes with it a wonderful sense of conviviality; meaning this place could be — should be — somewhere for people to interact, meet and be together.”

P.250 Elevators framed by bespoke oak and linen-lined backlit bookshelves
P.253–255 Cantilevered staircase by Tara Bernerd is crafted from limestone with metal and leather-wrapped handrail. Concierge desk sculpted from Ceppo stone and timber

& COMPANY 20 Years of Discovery
Flowers and Herbs of Early America
Watercolors by Finn Juhl

"We looked at how the exterior landscaping could speak to the interior and how to frame the lobby and the reception. I had in my mind that it should feel like my own home in Osaka, an approachable place for entertaining and socializing, therefore it needed to be fresh and light in approach, its tonality, texture and materials."

P.256 Main reception living room features an inset, bespoke encaustic tile floor and communal table with live timber edge
P.259 Upholstered banquette seating and side tables, crafted in walnut and limestone designed by Tara Bernerd

Six Senses Milan Brera

In Brera, Milan's artistic quarter—where neoclassical façades frame cobbled streets alive with galleries, boutiques, and restaurants—a 1950s landmark opposite the Pinacoteca di Brera has been reimagined as a Six Senses hotel and spa owned by Gruppo Statuto, with interior architecture and design by Tara Bernerd. With Bernerd's instinctive and experiential vision interwoven with the Six Senses signature ethos of wellness, sustainability and sensory richness, the studio has designed a retreat through a distinctly Milanese lens, inspired by the city's architectural and fashion heritage. Immersive and quietly luxurious, there are light-touch design cues and unexpected surprises throughout. A marble-clad juice bar offers glamorous cocktail-bar vibes; the open kitchen is framed by glazing for guests to view the action; carefully orchestrated communal seating feels intimate and refined. Marble surfaces, soft diffused lighting, and traditional Italian design gestures such as geometric motifs, leather privacy screens, sculpted banquettes, and timber wall profiles reference the studio's skill at creating crafted and materially rich spaces. Adding to a sense of escape is a semi-enclosed, verdant courtyard garden to the back. Below ground, the spa channels a contemporary, elemental calm. Rough-hewn Botticino marble contrasts with smooth travertine; mood-rich lighting sets the tone for restorative rituals. Alongside treatment rooms, thermal zones, and a travertine-lined pool is a Biohack chamber for innovative wellness with infusions and zero-gravity loungers. The 69 guest rooms and suites, designed with a soft color palette, take on the studio's signature modern approach to tactility, attention infused with Italian flair. Fluted oak headboards, rich upholstery, parquet oak flooring, and Murano glass lighting are offset by handcrafted details such as leather-wrapped minibar handles and cast glass wardrobe pulls, produced locally. The refined bathrooms, finished in Cipollino marble and Calacatta Oro, offer a restrained timeless luxury. The penthouse guest suite and function space with a generous wrap-around terrace and private pool add a generous feeling of escapism to this otherwise urban context.

P.262 CGI views of the reception, restaurant and penthouse suite

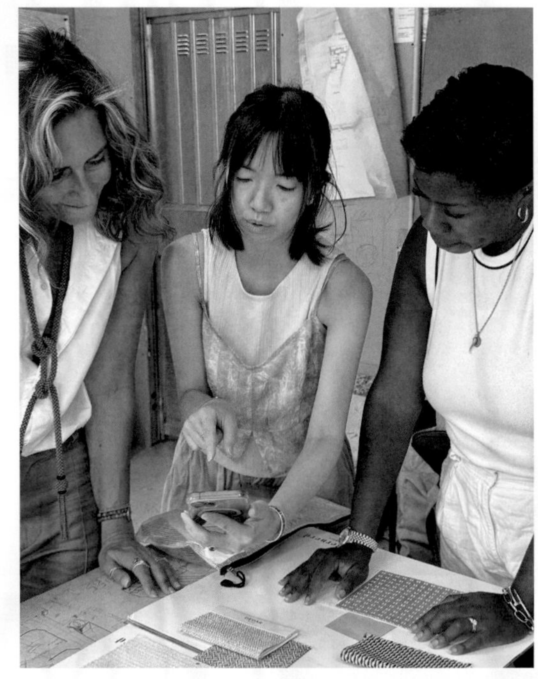

P.264–265 CGIs of guest rooms and public areas; Tara Bernerd with team. Site photos

GHISA

"Milan is the beginning of my next journey and Brera is my first stop. Working on this project has touched me deeply and awoken a new chapter in my design journey."

P.266 CGIs of guest bathroom, the spa; Tara Bernerd and team

Acknowledgments

My heartfelt thanks and dedication to the book squad: Lucien Smith, Nina Sanderson, and Lily Showering. This journey would not be possible without them and the efforts of my entire studio.

With deep acknowledgment to my directors: Dimos Giorgou, Adam Davies, Sophie Deeley, and Tommy Gymnander and associates: Colin McCole, Sam Lo Mingshum, Yuki Leung, Francesco Baiera, Louise Pittas, Alfred Yeung, Finn Foxcroft, and all the brilliant project leads and designers at TB&P.

Thanks also to writer Becky Sunshine, art director Micha Weidmann, my marvellous publisher Charles Miers and editor Ian Luna at Rizzoli, a constant source of inspiration.

For their support over the years, thanks to:

The Schörghuber Family

Rosewood Hotels & Resorts

Sonia Cheng

Radha Arora

Trish Luyckx

Dr Aron Harilela of Harilela Hotels

Belmond

Dan Ruff

Stephen Ross and Ken Himmel of Related Ross

Frank Gehry

Conrad Hotels & Resorts

Harvey Spevak

Barry Widen

Joe Pobanz

Filippo Arnaboldi of Frette and all the Frette family

Luigi Tagliabue and Andrea Tagliabue of Medea 1905

My dear friend Anton Bilton of Sabina Estates

Chris Norton and his introduction to the visionary Nadim Ashi and his wife Marlene of Fort Partners

Alejandro Reynal, Four Seasons Hotels and Resorts

Justin Hui and Jonathan Hui

Costas Spiliadis of Estiatorio Milos

Takashi Kobayashi and Daisuke Yoshihara of Palace Hotel Tokyo

Dottore Giuseppe Statuto of Gruppo Statuto, with deep respect and thanks

Ivan Statuto

Carlo Gallia

Six Senses Hotels

Neil Jacobs, a constant source of inspiration

Jon Paul Pérez and Nick Pérez, for their incredible support

St Regis Hotels & Resorts

Mandarin Oriental Hotel Group

Camilo Miguel Jr, Mast Capital

Barry Sternlicht, Starwood Capital Group

Rem Berg, Jondal

Tyler Brûlé, my inspiration and dear friend

Matthew Westerman

Norman and Elena Foster, for their support

Lubna Olayan, my mentor

The El Tanani Family

Kirsty Bertarelli

Jason Pomeranc, for giving me that first kick

Tamara Beckwith Veroni, for always being there

Geoffrey and Loulou Moore, for their friendship and support

Drew Goldman and Dana Farrington

Jay Jopling

Luca Finardi, for his friendship and support

Andrea Obertello

Stephanie Greger

Judy Dobias

Mustafa Salah, for helping me stay on the journey

All of this is made possible with the support of my family: my marvellous "Mr Fox" my husband, Tommy Foxcroft, and my brilliant stepson, Robert Foxcroft

With thanks to my loving mother, Susan Bernerd, and my father, Elliott Bernerd, who taught me how to be brave

Artwork credits:
Cesar Mendoza, Massimo Micheluzzi, Double Decker, Hanne Kroll, Helena Parada Kim, Zé Otavio, Michael Mann, Thomas Trum, Olaf Hajek, A Space for Art, Pontone Gallery, Matteo Massagrande, Rado Kirov, Do Min, Lee Leenam, Lee Jeonglok, JIHI, Kim Bumsu, Sweeney Co. Art Advisors, Ricardo Mazal, Raquel Charabati & Monica Rivera Rio Rocha, Javier Reyes, Carlos Hernandez Cruz, Maria Margarita Montaño Guerrero, Tatar Art Projects, Jeremie St-Onge – Verre D'Onge, Studio Alvo, MAGMA Gallery Officina Antiquaria, Sarah Miller and Partners, Gloria Estefanell Jara, Tappan Collective, Nik Wheeler / Wheeler Collective, Marc Gabor, Sara Marlowe Hall, Gabrielle Teschner, Sepideh Ilsley, Annelie Vandendael, Daigo Kamisuki of Crosslink Corporation

Photography credits:
Philip Vile pp. 6, 10, 14, 20, 24, 34, 35, 40, 41, 43, 44, 45, 46, 47, 126, 129, 130, 131, 133, 134–5, 136, 137, 138–9, 141, 142–3, 144, 145, 147, 148–9, 150, 151, 153, 154–5, 156, 157, 158, 161, 162–3, 164, 165, 166, 168, 169, 170, 202, 205, 206, 209, 210, 212–3, 214, 215, 216, 218, 219, 220, 222, Christopher Button Photography pp. 6, Tara Bernerd pp. 6, 8, 10, 14, 15, 16, 264, 265, 266, Alexis Armanet p. 10, Børge Mogensen for Fredericia p. 12, Jeanloup Sieff p. 12, Maison de Verre p. 14, Sanguer p. 15, Joep Verbeeten p. 15, Filippo Pincolini, Courtesy of Nilufar p. 15, Christophe Coënon Photographe p. 16, Martin Molcan p. 16 Davide Lovatti pp. 22–23, 26–27, 29, 30–31, 32, 36–37, 38–39, 48–49, 51, 52–53, Dennis Lo, Digital Lapin pp. 54, 56–57, 59, 60, 62–63, 65, 66–67, 69, 70–71, 72–73, 75, 76, 77, 78, 224, 226–7, 229, 230–1, 232, 235, William Jess Laird, Cover, pp. 82–83, 85, 86–87, 89, 90–91, 92, 94, 95, 96, 98–99, 100, 104–5, 108, 109, 110, 115, 116, 118–9, 120, 121, 122–3, 124–5, Lizzet Ortiz p. 97, Jenny Quicksall p. 80, Victor Stonem pp. 102–3, Edgardo Contreras pp. 107, 112–13, 114, Kate Martin pp. 172, 174–5, 176, 177, 179, 180, Ana Lui pp. 12, 182, 184–5, 186–7, 189, 191, 192–3, 194, 195, 196–7, 198–9, 201, Bronwyn Knight pp. 236, 239, 240–1, 243, 244–5, 246, Stirling Elmendorf Photography pp. 248, 250–1, 253, 254–5, 256–7, 259, 260–1, Tara Bernerd & Partners CGI pp. 262, 264, 266

First published in the United States of America in 2026 by Rizzoli International Publications, Inc.
49 West 27th Street
New York, NY 10001
www.rizzoliusa.com

Tara Bernerd:
A Design Journey

For Tara Bernerd & Partners

Editor: Lucien Smith
Editorial Coordination: Nina Sanderson
Editorial Assistance: Lily Showering
Front cover image: © William Jess Laird

Art Direction and Book Design by Micha Weidmann Studio

For Rizzoli International Publications, Inc.

Publisher: Charles Miers
Editor: Ian Luna
Project Editor: Joe Davidson
Production: Barbara Sadick & Eugene Lee
Proofreader: Mary Ellen Wilson

Printed in Singapore

2026 2027 2028 2029 2030 / 10987654321

ISBN: 978-0-8478-7645-7

The authorized representative in the EU for product safety and compliance is Mondadori Libri S.P.A., via Gian Battista Vico 42, Milan, Italy, 20123
www.mondadori.it

Visit us online
Instagram: @RizzoliBooks
Facebook.com/RizzoliNewYork
Youtube.com/user/RizzoliNY